CELEBRATING
GROUNDHOG DAY

CELEBRATING

GROUNDHOG DAY

History, Traditions, and Activities
A HOLIDAY BOOK FOR KIDS

Karen Bush Gibson

Illustrated by Monika Filipina

ROCKRIDGE
PRESS

First Rockridge Press hardcover edition 2022

Originally published in trade paperback by Rockridge Press 2021

Rockridge Press and the Rockridge Press logo are trademarks or registered trademarks of Callisto Media Inc. and/or its affiliates in the United States and other countries and may not be used without written permission.

For general information on our other products and services, please contact our Customer Care Department within the United States at (866) 744-2665, or outside the United States at (510) 253-0500.

Hardcover ISBN: 979-8-88650-448-4 | Paperback ISBN: 978-1-64739-767-8

eBook ISBN: 978-1-64739-768-5

Manufactured in the United States of America

Series Designer: Elizabeth Zuhl
Interior and Cover Designer: Francesca Pacchini
Art Producer: Tom Hood
Editor: Elizabeth Baird
Production Editor: Jenna Dutton
Production Manager: Martin Worthington

Illustration © Monika Filipina, 2021. Illustrator portrait courtesy of Chris Rout

10 9 8 7 6 5 4 3 2 1 0

If we had no winter, the spring
would not be so pleasant.
—Anne Bradstreet

CONTENTS

WHAT IS GROUNDHOG DAY?

Imagine a cold winter day. Frost covers the ground. A chill is in the air. An icy wind blows, making people pull their coats closer to their bodies. A day like this might make you wonder: When will the warm, sunny days of spring arrive?

People in the United States and Canada look for the answer to that question every February 2. And the answer comes from an unusual place: a furry groundhog!

Perhaps the most famous groundhog, or **marmot**, lives underground in a **burrow** in Punxsutawney, Pennsylvania. People all over the country know him as Punxsutawney Phil.

Tradition says that if Phil sees his shadow when he comes out of his burrow on February 2, there will be six more weeks of winter. But if he doesn't see his shadow, it means spring is coming. Most people hope Phil doesn't see his shadow. What about you?

Groundhog Day has been an American holiday for more than 100 years. But the tradition of celebrating the arrival of spring goes back thousands of years. Have you ever wondered how Groundhog Day got started? Or just how a groundhog got the job of predicting spring? Read on to find out!

HISTORY AND FOLKLORE

Many holidays have their beginnings in religious **traditions** from thousands of years ago. Groundhog Day is one of those holidays.

One kind of religion that celebrated a holiday at the beginning of February was **paganism**. Pagan festivals were common in **Celtic** countries like Ireland and Scotland. One of these festivals was called *Imbolc*.

Imbolc, one of four seasonal festivals, marked the beginning of spring. It celebrated the days growing longer and the first signs of new life. People celebrated with hearth fires, **bonfires**, and special foods. It was a time to prepare for growth and renewal. It was also a time to celebrate the goddess Brigid.

Meanwhile, people who practiced Christianity had their own celebrations in early February. The main holiday was celebrated about 40 days after Christmas.

It had different names, but became best known as *Candlemas*. On the second day of February, people brought candles to church. The candles were blessed by priests.

Families moved through the streets with their lit candles, happy to bring blessings back to their homes for the year. Lights from torches lit the way.

A folk song about Candlemas went something like this:

If Candlemas be fair and bright,
Come, Winter, have another flight;
If Candlemas brings clouds and rain,
Go Winter, and come not again.

This led to the beginnings of a legend. A sunny Candlemas meant winter would last longer. But a cloudy day meant an early spring was on its way.

Another sign of spring is the awakening of hibernating animals from their winter's sleep. People in Germany chose one of these, the hedgehog, to **predict** the arrival of spring. If this spiny mammal saw his shadow on Candlemas, they knew to expect six more weeks of winter. But if no shadow appeared, spring was on the way.

Groundhogs go by different names depending on where they live. They might be called "woodchucks," "land beavers," "mousebears," or even "whistle pigs."

In the 1800s, Germans joined people from other countries in moving to the United States. One area where many German **immigrants** settled was Pennsylvania. These people brought many traditions to their new home, including Candlemas.

However, there were no hedgehogs in North America. The settlers looked around and found another critter living in Pennsylvania: the groundhog!

Still, February 2 didn't become the holiday known as Groundhog Day until almost the end of the 1800s.

Many animals are less active in winter. But a groundhog's body temperature and heart rate drop dramatically. During hibernation, a groundhog's body temperature can drop from about 99 degrees Fahrenheit to as low as 37. The groundhog's breathing drops from about 16 breaths a minute to 2. And the heart rate can slow to 5 beats a minute from its usual 80.

On February 2, 1887, a group of men who belonged to the Punxsutawney Groundhog Club walked to a place called Gobbler's Knob. They pulled a groundhog from his burrow. The groundhog saw his shadow, predicting six more weeks of winter. And the groundhog was right!

Groundhog Day became a holiday in Pennsylvania. It soon spread throughout the United States and Canada. To this day, people still celebrate by gathering at Gobbler's Knob to see if Punxsutawney Phil will see his shadow or not, and to learn if there will be six more weeks of winter or an early spring.

HOW TO CELEBRATE

VISIT PUNXSUTAWNEY

Pennsylvania sees more snow than many other states do. In fact, February is one of the coldest months of the year there. But that doesn't stop 20,000 people from visiting every February.

People travel to Punxsutawney, a small town in western Pennsylvania, to see Punxsutawney Phil make his prediction about the end of winter. Does that sound like something you would like to do?

Celebrants who travel to Punxsutawney must wake up early on Groundhog Day. That's because they need to be at Gobbler's Knob before the Sun rises. Gobbler's Knob is a small, quiet, wooded area on top of a hill. This is where Punxsutawney Phil comes out to look for his shadow after sunrise.

On February 2, Punxsutawney Phil is the most popular animal in Pennsylvania. Gobbler's Knob has the biggest Groundhog Day celebration in the country. It usually lasts for a few days.

When not predicting seasons at Gobbler's Knob, Punxsutawney Phil lives with three other groundhogs in a heated area of the children's section of the Punxsutawney Memorial Library.

WATCH PUNXSUTAWNEY PHIL

Don't worry if you can't visit Punxsutawney on Groundhog Day. You can also see Punxsutawney Phil on television. Many television stations have cameras at the celebration at Gobbler's Knob.

The best way for most people to see Punxsutawney Phil is on a national morning news show. Reporters know that people all over the country want to see Punxsutawney Phil come out of his burrow. If you don't want to miss it, make sure to wake up early. Morning news shows may start as early as 6:00 a.m. Eastern Standard Time (EST).

Sometimes, there is a number to text that will deliver Phil's prediction. Ask your parents to text the number from their phone.

If you miss seeing Phil this year, don't worry! This famous groundhog also goes on talk shows and has appeared in the movies. One year, Punxsutawney Phil even visited the president.

LOOK FOR GROUNDHOG BOOKS AND NATURE SHOWS

You can also prepare for and celebrate Groundhog Day by reading books about groundhogs from libraries or bookstores. If you can't find anything about groundhogs, try looking for books about woodchucks instead. "Woodchuck" is another common name for groundhogs.

Ask your family or friends to join you in reading about groundhogs and Groundhog Day. Let people choose their favorite books. Maybe your library or classroom will have a special groundhog story time.

Nature channels also have special programs about groundhogs. Animal Planet has a show called *A Groundhog Day Story*. If you can't find it on television, ask an adult to help you check the Animal Planet website. PBS has a show called *Nature* that sometimes features groundhogs. Check your television listings.

VISIT GROUNDHOGS AT THE ZOO

Groundhogs are fascinating animals. They also live at zoos. Zoos can be excellent places to learn more about these marmots, like what their homes look like—groundhog burrows have lots of tunnels. The tunnels lead to a large chamber where groundhogs sleep.

In captivity, the average groundhog lives about 10 years. The Punxsutawney legend says that Phil is given a magic potion to live forever. Actually, there have been many new Punxsutawney Phils.

Gordy the Groundhog was about a year old when he moved to the Milwaukee Zoo in Wisconsin in 2019. In Massachusetts, the Zoo in Forest Park has a groundhog exhibit. Does your zoo have groundhogs? If not, they might have other tunnel digging mammals, like prairie dogs.

Remember, groundhogs like to settle down for long winter naps. You have a better chance of seeing them during spring, summer, and fall. Spring can be an especially active time for groundhogs. Baby groundhogs are often born in April.

LOOK FOR SIGNS OF SPRING

Groundhog Day is a way to celebrate the arrival of spring. Many people look forward to the warmer days of spring after the long, cold days of winter. What are some signs of spring where you live?

Flowers like crocuses and daffodils bloom early. Look for little green shoots pushing up from the dirt outside. Check the branches of trees. Look for little buds forming on the tree branches. These buds will turn into new leaves. On some trees, they will turn into flowers before turning into leaves.

Stop and listen. Do you hear the sounds of birds? Birds start chirping and singing with the return of spring. Bees and butterflies may start flying around, too. They're out looking for food.

Is there a pond in your town? Look for small bubbles floating in the water. These might be eggs that frogs lay. Soon those bubbles will be tadpoles.

AROUND THE WORLD

People have been trying to predict the weather for a very long time. All around the world, there are many traditions and celebrations about the weather.

Phil isn't the only groundhog who makes predictions about when spring will arrive. In New Jersey, Milltown Mel checks for his shadow every February. Wisconsin has Jimmy the Groundhog. Jimmy bit the mayor's ear one year, but he's been forgiven! Ohio has Buckeye Chuck, and Potomac Phil makes the predictions in Washington, DC. People in Georgia pay attention to General Beauregard Lee.

Groundhogs live in the central and eastern United States, as well as in southern Canada. In other parts of the country, people look to other animals to predict the arrival of spring. Mojave Maxine, a desert tortoise, makes predictions in Southern California. In central Texas, they have Beecave Bob. Bob is an armadillo,

Jimmy
SUN PRAIRIE, WI

Buckeye Chuck
MARION, OH

Punxsutawney Phil
PUNXSUTAWNEY, PA

Milltown Mel
MILLTOWN, NJ

Potomac Phil
WASHINGTON, DC

General Beauregard Lee
JACKSON, GA

the state animal of Texas. Some Texans celebrate Armadillo Day on February 2.

Canadians celebrate Groundhog Day, too. But they do it with Wiarton Willie, a white groundhog who lives in Wiarton, Ontario. Because Canada is so far north, their winters are very long. People in Wiarton have to wake up Willie from **hibernation** on February 2 to make a prediction. Afterward, there's a parade and a pancake breakfast.

Like the United States, Canada is a very large country, so it has a few different groundhogs who pop up on Groundhog Day. While Willie is the best known, there's Balzac Billy, from Balzac, Alberta, as well as Winnipeg Willow in Winnipeg, Manitoba, and Fred la Marmotte. Fred lives in the French-speaking province of Quebec.

Other countries have different weather- and season-related celebrations to mark the coming of spring. Some of them might even seem familiar to you. Do you remember learning about Imbolc earlier in this book? St. Brigid's Day is the modern name for Imbolc, and it's still celebrated in Ireland! One tradition is that a wet St. Brigid's Day (February 1) is followed by a dry spring. But if it's dry on St. Brigid's Day, a rainy spring will follow.

Groundhog teeth grow about 1/16 of an inch each week.

Another St. Brigid's Day tradition is to leave a cloth or scarf outside the night before. It is believed that St. Brigid will pass by and bless the cloth. People later use this special cloth to cure sore throats or headaches.

Hindus in northern India celebrate the end of winter and beginning of spring with a burst of color. The March festival is called Holi. During Holi, people throw colored powder at each other! The joyful day symbolizes spring's many colors and new beginnings.

While many weather- and season-related traditions happen in early February, other celebrations happen at different times of the year.

In South America, the Indigenous people of Peru and Bolivia believe that if the stars in the Pleiades constellation shine brightly during June, then there will be plentiful rainfall during the growing season that lasts from October to May.

Germany has a tradition called Seven Sleepers Day. If it rains on June 27, there will be seven more weeks of rain, or a rainier summer overall. A sunny day without rain means it will be a sunny summer.

A similar day is St. Swithin's Day in the United Kingdom. If it rains on July 15, it will rain for the next 40 days and nights. If it does not rain, fair weather is expected. There's even a rhyme:

> *St. Swithin's day if you do rain*
> *For 40 days it will remain*
> *St. Swithin's day if you be fair*
> *For 40 days it will rain no more.*

Traditions can be a lot of fun, don't you think?

DIGGING DEEPER

Each year, people wait in excitement for Punxsutawney Phil's prediction. But is his prediction correct? For the past 10 years, he's been right about 40 percent of the time. That means he's wrong more often than he's right.

Some years, Punxsutawney Phil is both right and wrong. How can that be? Because the weather can be very different in different parts of the country.

The United States has different climates. **Climate** is what the weather is like over long periods of time. In some parts of the United States, the climate is hot and dry all year—even during the winter! In other parts of the United States, the weather changes with the seasons.

Even though Punxsutawney Phil is wrong sometimes, Groundhog Day is still fun to celebrate. Many people look forward to spring every year. They get so excited for the start of spring that they pay attention to predictions, even from large ground squirrels like the groundhog.

Our planet moves through four seasons every year: spring, summer, autumn (or fall), and winter.

Seasons happen as the Earth rotates around the Sun. And if you look at a globe, you'll see that the Earth is tilted. The North Pole doesn't point straight up. It actually tilts 23.5 degrees.

This means different places on Earth are closer to the Sun during certain times of the year. In the United States, those times are spring and summer. More sunlight helps plants grow. When spring arrives, trees put out new leaves and flowers start to blossom. By summer, the trees are full of leaves, and sunset is later in the evening.

When autumn comes, it means your part of the Earth is starting to move away from the Sun. There is less light. Leaves on trees begin to change color. Winter has the least amount of light. The Sun sets much earlier in the day. Leaves fall from most trees.

The seasons and Groundhog Day are connected to astronomy. Astronomy is the study of space and objects like the Earth, Moon, and Sun.

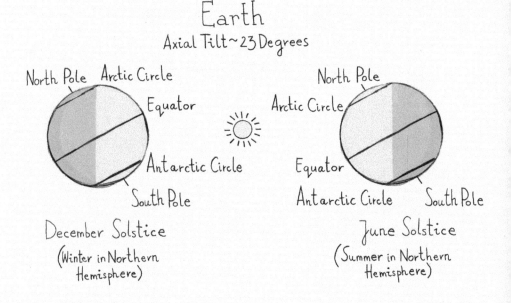

Earth
Axial Tilt ~ 23 Degrees

North Pole Arctic Circle
Equator
Antarctic Circle
South Pole
December Solstice
(Winter in Northern Hemisphere)

North Pole
Arctic Circle
Equator
Antarctic Circle South Pole
June Solstice
(Summer in Northern Hemisphere)

Groundhog Day is what is known as a cross-quarter day. A cross-quarter day is the midway point between a **solstice** and an **equinox**.

A solstice happens when the Sun is highest in the sky (summer) and when it's lowest in the sky (winter). An equinox also happens twice a year, during the spring and fall. It's when the amount of daylight and darkness are equal. Seasons start on the first day of a solstice or an equinox.

There are four cross-quarter days during the year. Groundhog Day is one of them. It is midway between the winter solstice and the spring equinox.

The next cross-quarter day falls on May Day, which is celebrated in some parts of the world.

Summer's cross-quarter day falls on the first day of August. The autumn cross-quarter day is also connected to a holiday you might be familiar with: Halloween!

Nature has many ways of letting people know about the changing seasons and weather. If you look closely, you'll see clues.

Perhaps one of the biggest clues is hibernation. Some mammals know it will be harder for them to find food during the winter, so they decide to hibernate. During hibernation, animals save their energy by being still. Their body temperature drops, and they don't need as much food as they would if they were awake. This helps them survive during the winter.

Many animals that hibernate live in burrows, like groundhogs and chipmunks. They eat a lot during autumn to prepare for hibernation.

Hibernating animals "wake," or become more active, when spring gets close. Their bodies tell them food is plentiful. You'll tend to see more active animals in the spring.

Many animals are born in the spring, too. Deer, black bears, and, yes, even groundhogs are often born in the spring.

There are many animals that do not hibernate, but they still give clues about the changing seasons. Birds give lots of clues. In North America, birds **migrate** in spring and fall.

As temperatures drop in autumn, many birds, such as geese, migrate south. They are flying to warmer weather. Warmer weather usually means there will be more food for them to eat, like plants, berries, and bugs.

When the weather warms up, crickets start chirping. Count the number of cricket chirps in 15 seconds. Add that number to 37, and you have a good guess about the outside temperature.

Birds can give clues about the day-to-day weather, too. Have you ever noticed birds flying closer to the ground just before rain? When rain is coming, the air becomes heavy. This makes it harder for birds to fly as high.

One species of bird, the swallow, has sensitive ears. They can feel the drop in air pressure. Flying lower is easier when air pressure drops. Many people see low-flying birds as a sign of rain.

CULTURE CORNER

GROUNDHOG MASK

Would you like to see the world as a groundhog? Now's your chance! Make this mask to wear on Groundhog Day. You can pretend to be a groundhog looking for your shadow.

MATERIALS

Plain white or light-colored paper

Scissors

Thick paper, such as construction paper, card stock, paper plates, or thin cardboard

Crayons or markers

A hole punch or pencil

2 pieces of string or ribbon, each about 6 inches long

1. Draw or trace a copy of this groundhog mask on a sheet of plain white paper.

2. Cut out your mask. Don't forget to cut out the eyes!

3. Place the mask pattern on thick paper. Trace around the pattern.

4. Cut out your mask from the thick paper or thin cardboard.

5. Use crayons or markers to decorate your mask. Maybe you'll want to give it some whiskers. What color is the nose?

6. Using a hole punch, punch small holes about half an inch from each side.

7. Thread each string through a hole on the side of the mask. Knot it on the front side of the mask.

8. Put on your mask. Tie the ends of the two strings behind your head. Ask a sibling, friend, or parent for help if you are having trouble!

GROUNDHOG DAY PREDICTIONS

The Groundhog Day legend uses predictions. Successful predictions are often the result of recognizing patterns.

Meteorologists make predictions called **forecasts**. These predictions are based on experience and understanding of weather patterns. Other predictions, like whether spring will come early if Punxsutawney Phil doesn't see his shadow, are just guesses. Making predictions and finding out whether you're right can be fun. As you get ready for Groundhog Day this year, see if your family, friends, or classmates would like to make predictions about if Phil will see his shadow or not!

Makes: one poster and 10 groundhog heads

MATERIALS

Poster board	**Scissors**
Markers	**Glue**
Brown construction paper	**Tape**

1. Draw a groundhog in the middle of the poster board (you can trace the illustration on the next page, or use it as a guide). Write these words nearby: *Will I see my shadow?*

2. On one side of the groundhog, near the top, write: *I think he will see his shadow. Six more weeks of winter.*

3. On the other side of the groundhog, write: *I think he will NOT see his shadow. Spring is coming.*

4. Cut out 10 large circles from the construction paper. Trace something like a bowl.

5. Cut out 20 smaller circles from the construction paper. Trace something like a cup or can.

6. Add glue to the bottom half of the small circles. Stick them on the back of the larger circle to make ears.

7. Draw on eyes, nose, and a mouth, or let your friends and family decorate the heads.

8. Hand out a groundhog head to friends and family along with a piece of tape. Ask them to make a prediction about whether the groundhog will see his shadow. Have them tape their groundhog under the statement they agree with.

9. Which prediction got the most votes? How many predictions were correct?

SHADOW EXPERIMENT

Punxsutawney Phil's prediction about spring comes from whether he sees his shadow on February 2. Shadows are made when an object blocks light. The only way to see a groundhog's shadow is on a sunny day, because the groundhog's body blocks the light from the Sun.

Three things are needed to make a shadow: light, an object to block light, and a surface for the shadow. When the Sun is in front of an object, a shadow forms behind the object.

Shadows are interesting. Have you ever noticed that sometimes your shadow is gigantic? Other times, it's small. Sometimes it's a skinny shadow. Other times, it's thick. This is because of where the light is when it hits an object. You can keep track of the shape and size of your own shadow! All you need is some sunlight, some chalk, and a friend to help.

---

1. Pick an outdoor spot like a sidewalk or driveway that gets sunlight all day.

2. Early in the morning, go outside to the spot with your helper. Mark the spot where you're standing with chalk. Have your helper trace your shadow with one color of chalk.

3. Two hours later, return to the same spot. Have your helper trace your shadow again with a different color of chalk.

4. Every two or three hours, return to the same spot and have your helper trace your shadow with a different color of chalk.

5. After the last shadow is drawn, compare the shadows traced at different times. How did they change? Why do you think they changed?

A NATURE WALK

Many groundhogs making predictions in the United States and Canada live in protected areas. These might be parks where they are fed and kept safe. Other groundhogs live in zoos. But many groundhogs and other marmots live in the wild.

Taking a nature walk in a wilderness area or state park can be a little bit like being a detective, especially if you look for clues about animals and their **habitats**.

Groundhogs like to live in open spaces, like fields and clearings in forests. They live underground in burrows. This keeps them safe from other animals and gives them a place to hibernate.

Look for grassy areas with short plants. Groundhogs eat plants. They also eat insects, leaves, and bark from trees. Can you spot any trees with missing bark?

Do you see small piles of dirt? This could mean a nearby burrow. Groundhogs can move more than 700 pounds of soil when they dig their burrows.

The entrance to a groundhog burrow is a hole about the size of a small plate. It's hard to see very far inside the burrows, but you can use your imagination. Just like people, groundhogs have a room for sleeping. They use another room for their bathroom.

Groundhogs aren't the only animals that live in burrows. Gophers, rats, badgers, and rabbits are some of the many animals that live in burrows.

It's very important to remember that you should never stick your hand or anything else in a burrow. That scares whatever animal lives there. And scared animals bite!

Burrows can be up to 6 feet deep and 20 feet long. They usually have at least two entrances.

GROUNDHOG DAY COOKIES

Will the groundhog see its shadow or not? You can be ready with these cookies that show the groundhog peeping out of his burrow on Groundhog Day. Ask an adult to help you make these sweet treats!

Makes: one dozen cookies

INGREDIENTS

½ cup salted butter

½ cup milk

1 cup light brown sugar, packed

1 cup granulated sugar

¼ cup cocoa power

⅔ cup peanut butter*

1 ½ teaspoons vanilla extract

Chocolate taffy candies

3-ounce bottle sprinkles (white or multicolor would work best)

1. Prepare two cookie sheets by lining them with parchment or wax paper.

2. In a saucepan, mix the butter, milk, brown sugar, granulated sugar, and cocoa powder. Cook on the stovetop over low heat for 3 to 5 minutes. Stir the ingredients with a long-handled wooden or silicone spoon until the butter melts.

3. After the butter melts, increase the heat to medium. Bring to a boil, stirring constantly, for about 1 minute.

4. Remove the pan from the heat and stir until the mixture stops bubbling.

5. Add the peanut butter and vanilla. Stir until melted and combined with the other ingredients.

6. Add the oats and mix well.

7. Drop scoops of 1 to 2 tablespoons of dough on cookie sheets 1 inch apart.

8. Soften a chocolate taffy candy by rolling it between your hands. Mold the candy into the top half of a groundhog.

9. Stick the bottom of each groundhog into a cookie mound while the cookies are still warm.

10. Use sprinkles to make the eyes and mouth on each groundhog.

11. Let the cookies cool for about 30 minutes. The cookies will harden around the groundhogs.

If someone is allergic to peanut butter, you can replace it with almond or sunflower seed butter.

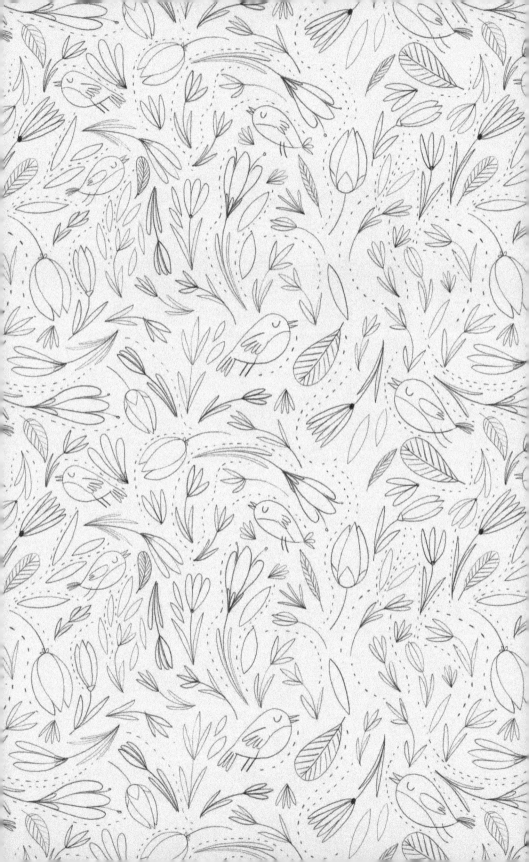

GLOSSARY

bonfires (BON-fires): Large outdoor fires

burrow (BUR-oh): A tunnel or hole in the ground made and lived in by some animals

Celtic (KEL-tik): The languages and cultures of Ireland, Scotland, Wales, Cornwall, the Isle of Man, and Brittany

climate (KLYE-mit): The usual weather in a place

equinox (EE-kwa-noks): Two days during the year when day and night last the same amount of time

forecasts (FOR-kasts): Saying what will happen in the future, usually about weather

habitat (HAB-uh-tat): The place and conditions where an animal or plant lives

hibernation (hye-bur-NAY-shun): When certain animals spend winter in a deep sleep in order to survive

immigrants (IM-uh-grents): People who come to live permanently in a foreign country

marmot (MAR-mut): A burrowing rodent found in North America, Europe, and north Asia

migrate (MYE-grate): To move to a different region or climate

paganism (PAY-guhn-izm): Often religions that worship many gods; not one of the world's main religions

predict (pri-DIKT): To make a guess about what will happen in the future

solstice (SOLE-stes): Two days during the year when the Sun reaches its highest or lowest point in the sky at noon; the longest and shortest days of the year

traditions (truh-DISH-uhns): Customs or beliefs that are handed down from one generation to the next

RESOURCES

National Geographic, **"10 Facts You Didn't Know**
about Groundhogs": NationalGeographic.com
/news/2014/1/groundhogs-day-animals-wildlife.

National Wildlife Federation, "On Groundhog
Day: Ten Things to Know about These Surprising
Creatures": Blog.NWF.org/2011/01/on-groundhog
-day-ten-things-to-know-about-these-surprising
-creatures.

PBS LearningMedia, "Groundhog Day":
PBSLearning
Media.org/resource/83dfbd1c-ef5b-4925-a225
-ff835bef4496/groundhog-day-all-about
-the-holidays.

VisitPA, "Groundhog Day": VisitPA.com/article
/groundhog-day.

The Punxsutawney Groundhog Club:
Groundhog.org.

ABOUT THE AUTHOR

Karen Bush Gibson has written dozens of children's books on many different subjects. She writes about people, places, and history. And like all groundhog watchers, she loves spring.

ABOUT THE ILLUSTRATOR

Monika Filipina has been passionate about drawing and children's books since she was very young. One day, she simply decided to pack her bags and move to the UK to study art. In 2014 she successfully completed a master's degree in children's book illustration at Cambridge School of Arts. She is now an award-winning illustrator, living and working in her hometown of Toruń, Poland.

Printed in the USA
CPSIA information can be obtained
at www.ICGtesting.com
CBHW042158150224
4326CB00001B/3